MW00884352

My
SOCCER
Season

A journal of my skills, my games, and my memories.

Karleen Tauszik

Text and layout copyright © 2018 by Karleen Tauszik
Cover Illustration from BigstockPhoto.com, photo 935748, contributor Gino Santa Maria
Cover Design Copyright © 2018 by Karleen Tauszik
Cover design and cover photo editing by Karleen Tauszik

All rights reserved, including the right of reproduction in whole or in part in any form.

Summary: This journal provides children with a place to track their soccer season: their games, practices, areas of improvement and contribution, and their fun memories.

ISBN-13: 978-1985624122
ISBN-10: 1985624125

Karleen Tauszik is the author of books for children ages 8-12. Visit her on the web at KarleenT.com, where you can see her other books and sign up for her newsletter.

This book belongs to

_____

My Soccer Season

from _____ to _____
          Date   Date

Hurrah! You're on the team!

This journal is the perfect place to track your soccer season—your practice sessions, your games, the highlights of the season, and all the fun you'll have.

Here's what you'll find inside:

First, there are four pages to journal your pre-season weeks of practice.

Next, there are enough pages to journal up to 35 games, so you have enough for preseason games, the main season, and a few for tournaments and postseason games. Need more? One is reserved for photocopying.

In between each game page, you'll find a page to journal how your practice sessions are going.

At the end, there are seven blank pages to fill with photos, extra notes, statistics, and mementos. You can even get all your teammates to write notes and their autographs if you like. Add whatever you want to so you remember your soccer season and make this book uniquely yours.

Good luck and have a great season!

Pre-Season Practice

The week starting _____

Day & Date

Coach's focus this week is: _____

_____

_____

My focus this week is: _____

_____

_____

How I feel starting out: _____

_____

_____

What I think I can contribute to the team this week: _____

_____

_____

My notes about this week's practice: _____

_____

_____

_____

_____

_____

_____

_____

Pre-Season Practice

The week starting _____
Day & Date

Coach's focus this week is: _____

_____

_____

My focus this week is: _____

_____

_____

How I feel starting out: _____

_____

_____

What I think I can contribute to the team this week: _____

_____

_____

My notes about this week's practice: _____

_____

_____

_____

_____

_____

_____

_____

Pre-Season Practice

The week starting _____

Coach's focus this week is: _____

_____

_____

My focus this week is: _____

_____

_____

How I feel starting out: _____

_____

_____

What I think I can contribute to the team this week: _____

_____

_____

My notes about this week's practice: _____

_____

_____

_____

_____

_____

_____

_____

Pre-Season Practice

The week starting _____
Day & Date

Coach's focus this week is: _____

_____

_____

My focus this week is: _____

_____

_____

How I feel starting out: _____

_____

_____

What I think I can contribute to the team this week: _____

_____

_____

My notes about this week's practice: _____

_____

_____

_____

_____

_____

_____

_____

Game Day

Game Date: _____ Game Time: _____

We played against: _____ Home ☐ Away ☐

Positions I played: _____ Final Score: _____

My summary: _____

_____

_____

_____

Coach's comments: _____

_____

_____

My contributions: _____

_____

_____

Where I could have done better: _____

_____

_____

Highlights of the game: _____

_____

_____

_____

_____

_____

Practice

Starting _____ until our next game on _____

Day & Date   Day & Date

Coach's focus this week is: _____

_____

_____

My focus this week is: _____

_____

_____

How I feel looking ahead: _____

_____

_____

What I think I can contribute to the team this week: _____

_____

_____

My notes about this week's practice: _____

_____

_____

_____

_____

_____

_____

_____

Game Day

Game Date: _____ Game Time: _____

We played against: _____ Home ☐   Away ☐

Positions I played: _____ Final Score: _____

My summary: _____

_____

_____

_____

Coach's comments: _____

_____

_____

My contributions: _____

_____

_____

Where I could have done better: _____

_____

_____

Highlights of the game: _____

_____

_____

_____

_____

Practice

Starting _____ until our next game on _____
                    Day & Date   Day & Date

Coach's focus this week is: _____

_____

_____

My focus this week is: _____

_____

_____

How I feel looking ahead: _____

_____

_____

What I think I can contribute to the team this week: _____

_____

_____

My notes about this week's practice: _____

_____

_____

_____

_____

_____

_____

_____

Game Day

Game Date: _____ Game Time: _____

We played against: _____ Home ☐   Away ☐

Positions I played: _____ Final Score: _____

My summary: _____

_____

_____

_____

Coach's comments: _____

_____

_____

My contributions: _____

_____

_____

_____

Where I could have done better: _____

_____

_____

_____

Highlights of the game: _____

_____

_____

_____

_____

Practice

Starting _____ until our next game on _____
Day & Date   Day & Date

Coach's focus this week is: _____

_____

_____

My focus this week is: _____

_____

_____

How I feel looking ahead: _____

_____

_____

What I think I can contribute to the team this week: _____

_____

_____

My notes about this week's practice: _____

_____

_____

_____

_____

_____

_____

_____

_____

Game Day

Game Date: _____ Game Time: _____

We played against: _____ Home ☐   Away ☐

Positions I played: _____ Final Score: _____

My summary: _____

_____

_____

_____

Coach's comments: _____

_____

_____

My contributions: _____

_____

_____

Where I could have done better: _____

_____

_____

Highlights of the game: _____

_____

_____

_____

_____

Practice

Starting _____ until our next game on _____

Day & Date   Day & Date

Coach's focus this week is: _____

_____

_____

My focus this week is: _____

_____

_____

How I feel looking ahead: _____

_____

_____

What I think I can contribute to the team this week: _____

_____

_____

My notes about this week's practice: _____

_____

_____

_____

_____

_____

_____

_____

Game Day

Game Date: _____ Game Time: _____

We played against: _____ Home ☐   Away ☐

Positions I played: _____ Final Score: _____

My summary: _____

_____

_____

_____

Coach's comments: _____

_____

_____

My contributions: _____

_____

_____

_____

Where I could have done better: _____

_____

_____

_____

Highlights of the game: _____

_____

_____

_____

_____

_____

Practice

Starting _____ until our next game on _____

Day & Date   Day & Date

Coach's focus this week is: _____

_____

_____

My focus this week is: _____

_____

_____

How I feel looking ahead: _____

_____

_____

What I think I can contribute to the team this week: _____

_____

_____

My notes about this week's practice: _____

_____

_____

_____

_____

_____

_____

_____

_____

Game Day

Game Date: _____ Game Time: _____

We played against: _____ Home ☐   Away ☐

Positions I played: _____ Final Score: _____

My summary: _____

_____

_____

_____

Coach's comments: _____

_____

_____

My contributions: _____

_____

_____

_____

Where I could have done better: _____

_____

_____

_____

Highlights of the game: _____

_____

_____

_____

_____

Practice

Starting _____ until our next game on _____
$\qquad\qquad$ Day & Date $\qquad\qquad\qquad\qquad\qquad\qquad\qquad\qquad$ Day & Date

Coach's focus this week is: _____

_____

_____

My focus this week is: _____

_____

_____

How I feel looking ahead: _____

_____

_____

What I think I can contribute to the team this week: _____

_____

_____

My notes about this week's practice: _____

_____

_____

_____

_____

_____

_____

_____

_____

Game Day

Game Date: _____ Game Time: _____

We played against: _____ Home ☐   Away ☐

Positions I played: _____ Final Score: _____

My summary: _____

_____

_____

_____

Coach's comments: _____

_____

_____

My contributions: _____

_____

_____

Where I could have done better: _____

_____

_____

Highlights of the game: _____

_____

_____

_____

_____

_____

Practice

Starting _____ until our next game on _____
Day & Date Day & Date

Coach's focus this week is: _____

_____

_____

My focus this week is: _____

_____

_____

How I feel looking ahead: _____

_____

_____

What I think I can contribute to the team this week: _____

_____

_____

My notes about this week's practice: _____

_____

_____

_____

_____

_____

_____

_____

Game Day

Game Date: _____ Game Time: _____

We played against: _____ Home ☐ Away ☐

Positions I played: _____ Final Score: _____

My summary: _____

_____

_____

_____

Coach's comments: _____

_____

_____

My contributions: _____

_____

_____

_____

Where I could have done better: _____

_____

_____

_____

Highlights of the game: _____

_____

_____

_____

_____

_____

Practice

Starting _____ until our next game on _____
Day & Date   Day & Date

Coach's focus this week is: _____

_____

_____

My focus this week is: _____

_____

_____

How I feel looking ahead: _____

_____

_____

What I think I can contribute to the team this week: _____

_____

_____

My notes about this week's practice: _____

_____

_____

_____

_____

_____

_____

_____

_____

Game Day

Game Date: _____ Game Time: _____

We played against: _____ Home ☐   Away ☐

Positions I played: _____ Final Score: _____

My summary: _____

_____

_____

_____

Coach's comments: _____

_____

_____

My contributions: _____

_____

_____

Where I could have done better: _____

_____

_____

Highlights of the game: _____

_____

_____

_____

_____

Practice

Starting _____ until our next game on _____
Day & Date   Day & Date

Coach's focus this week is: _____

_____

_____

My focus this week is: _____

_____

_____

How I feel looking ahead: _____

_____

_____

What I think I can contribute to the team this week: _____

_____

_____

My notes about this week's practice: _____

_____

_____

_____

_____

_____

_____

_____

_____

Game Day

Game Date: _____ Game Time: _____

We played against: _____ Home ☐   Away ☐

Positions I played: _____ Final Score: _____

My summary: _____

_____

_____

_____

Coach's comments: _____

_____

_____

My contributions: _____

_____

_____

Where I could have done better: _____

_____

_____

Highlights of the game: _____

_____

_____

_____

_____

Practice

Starting _____ until our next game on _____
                 Day & Date   Day & Date

Coach's focus this week is: _____

_____

_____

My focus this week is: _____

_____

_____

How I feel looking ahead: _____

_____

_____

What I think I can contribute to the team this week: _____

_____

_____

My notes about this week's practice: _____

_____

_____

_____

_____

_____

_____

_____

_____

Game Day

Game Date: _____   Game Time: _____

We played against: _____   Home ☐   Away ☐

Positions I played: _____   Final Score: _____

My summary: _____

_____

_____

_____

Coach's comments: _____

_____

_____

My contributions: _____

_____

_____

Where I could have done better: _____

_____

_____

Highlights of the game: _____

_____

_____

_____

_____

Practice

Starting _____ until our next game on _____
                 Day & Date   Day & Date

Coach's focus this week is: _____

_____

_____

My focus this week is: _____

_____

_____

How I feel looking ahead: _____

_____

_____

What I think I can contribute to the team this week: _____

_____

_____

My notes about this week's practice: _____

_____

_____

_____

_____

_____

_____

_____

Game Day

Game Date: _____ Game Time: _____

We played against: _____ Home ☐ Away ☐

Positions I played: _____ Final Score: _____

My summary: _____

_____

_____

_____

Coach's comments: _____

_____

_____

My contributions: _____

_____

_____

Where I could have done better: _____

_____

_____

Highlights of the game: _____

_____

_____

_____

_____

Practice

Starting _____ until our next game on _____

Day & Date   Day & Date

Coach's focus this week is: _____

_____

_____

My focus this week is: _____

_____

_____

How I feel looking ahead: _____

_____

_____

What I think I can contribute to the team this week: _____

_____

_____

My notes about this week's practice: _____

_____

_____

_____

_____

_____

_____

_____

_____

Game Day

Game Date: _____   Game Time: _____

We played against: _____   Home ☐   Away ☐

Positions I played: _____   Final Score: _____

My summary: _____

_____

_____

_____

Coach's comments: _____

_____

_____

My contributions: _____

_____

_____

Where I could have done better: _____

_____

_____

Highlights of the game: _____

_____

_____

_____

_____

Practice

Starting _____ until our next game on _____
    Day & Date   Day & Date

Coach's focus this week is: _____

_____

_____

My focus this week is: _____

_____

_____

How I feel looking ahead: _____

_____

_____

What I think I can contribute to the team this week: _____

_____

_____

My notes about this week's practice: _____

_____

_____

_____

_____

_____

_____

_____

_____

Game Day

Game Date: _____ Game Time: _____

We played against: _____ Home ☐   Away ☐

Positions I played: _____ Final Score: _____

My summary: _____

_____

_____

_____

Coach's comments: _____

_____

_____

My contributions: _____

_____

_____

Where I could have done better: _____

_____

_____

Highlights of the game: _____

_____

_____

_____

_____

Practice

Starting _____ until our next game on _____

Day & Date   Day & Date

Coach's focus this week is: _____

_____

_____

My focus this week is: _____

_____

_____

How I feel looking ahead: _____

_____

_____

What I think I can contribute to the team this week: _____

_____

_____

My notes about this week's practice: _____

_____

_____

_____

_____

_____

_____

_____

_____

Game Day

Game Date: _____ Game Time: _____

We played against: _____ Home ☐   Away ☐

Positions I played: _____ Final Score: _____

My summary: _____

_____

_____

_____

Coach's comments: _____

_____

_____

My contributions: _____

_____

_____

_____

Where I could have done better: _____

_____

_____

_____

Highlights of the game: _____

_____

_____

_____

_____

_____

Practice

Starting _____ until our next game on _____

Day & Date   Day & Date

Coach's focus this week is: _____

_____

_____

My focus this week is: _____

_____

_____

How I feel looking ahead: _____

_____

_____

What I think I can contribute to the team this week: _____

_____

_____

My notes about this week's practice: _____

_____

_____

_____

_____

_____

_____

_____

Game Day

Game Date: _____   Game Time: _____

We played against: _____   Home ☐   Away ☐

Positions I played: _____   Final Score: _____

My summary: _____

_____

_____

_____

Coach's comments: _____

_____

_____

My contributions: _____

_____

_____

Where I could have done better: _____

_____

_____

Highlights of the game: _____

_____

_____

_____

_____

_____

Practice

Starting _____ until our next game on _____
        Day & Date   Day & Date

Coach's focus this week is: _____

_____

_____

My focus this week is: _____

_____

_____

How I feel looking ahead: _____

_____

_____

What I think I can contribute to the team this week: _____

_____

_____

My notes about this week's practice: _____

_____

_____

_____

_____

_____

_____

_____

Game Day

Game Date: _____ Game Time: _____

We played against: _____ Home ☐   Away ☐

Positions I played: _____ Final Score: _____

My summary: _____

_____

_____

_____

Coach's comments: _____

_____

_____

My contributions: _____

_____

_____

_____

Where I could have done better: _____

_____

_____

_____

Highlights of the game: _____

_____

_____

_____

_____

Practice

Starting _____ until our next game on _____
         Day & Date   Day & Date

Coach's focus this week is: _____

_____

_____

My focus this week is: _____

_____

_____

How I feel looking ahead: _____

_____

_____

What I think I can contribute to the team this week: _____

_____

_____

My notes about this week's practice: _____

_____

_____

_____

_____

_____

_____

_____

_____

Game Day

Game Date: _____ Game Time: _____

We played against: _____ Home ☐   Away ☐

Positions I played: _____ Final Score: _____

My summary: _____

_____

_____

_____

Coach's comments: _____

_____

_____

My contributions: _____

_____

_____

_____

Where I could have done better: _____

_____

_____

_____

Highlights of the game: _____

_____

_____

_____

_____

_____

Practice

Starting _____ until our next game on _____

Day & Date   Day & Date

Coach's focus this week is: _____

_____

My focus this week is: _____

_____

How I feel looking ahead: _____

_____

What I think I can contribute to the team this week: _____

_____

My notes about this week's practice: _____

_____

_____

_____

_____

_____

_____

_____

Game Day

Game Date: _____   Game Time: _____

We played against: _____   Home ☐   Away ☐

Positions I played: _____   Final Score: _____

My summary: _____

_____

_____

_____

Coach's comments: _____

_____

_____

My contributions: _____

_____

_____

_____

Where I could have done better: _____

_____

_____

_____

Highlights of the game: _____

_____

_____

_____

_____

_____

Practice

Starting _____ until our next game on _____
Day & Date   Day & Date

Coach's focus this week is: _____

_____

My focus this week is: _____

_____

How I feel looking ahead: _____

_____

What I think I can contribute to the team this week: _____

_____

My notes about this week's practice: _____

_____

_____

_____

_____

_____

_____

_____

Game Day

Game Date: _____ Game Time: _____

We played against: _____ Home ☐   Away ☐

Positions I played: _____ Final Score: _____

My summary: _____

_____

_____

_____

Coach's comments: _____

_____

_____

My contributions: _____

_____

_____

Where I could have done better: _____

_____

_____

Highlights of the game: _____

_____

_____

_____

_____

_____

Practice

Starting _____ until our next game on _____
        Day & Date   Day & Date

Coach's focus this week is: _____

_____

_____

My focus this week is: _____

_____

_____

How I feel looking ahead: _____

_____

_____

What I think I can contribute to the team this week: _____

_____

_____

My notes about this week's practice: _____

_____

_____

_____

_____

_____

_____

_____

_____

Game Day

Game Date: _____ Game Time: _____

We played against: _____ Home ☐   Away ☐

Positions I played: _____ Final Score: _____

My summary: _____

_____

_____

_____

Coach's comments: _____

_____

_____

My contributions: _____

_____

_____

_____

Where I could have done better: _____

_____

_____

Highlights of the game: _____

_____

_____

_____

_____

Practice

Starting _____ until our next game on _____
                    Day & Date   Day & Date

Coach's focus this week is: _____

_____

_____

My focus this week is: _____

_____

_____

How I feel looking ahead: _____

_____

_____

What I think I can contribute to the team this week: _____

_____

_____

My notes about this week's practice: _____

_____

_____

_____

_____

_____

_____

_____

_____

Game Day

Game Date: _____   Game Time: _____

We played against: _____ Home ☐   Away ☐

Positions I played: _____ Final Score: _____

My summary: _____

_____

_____

_____

Coach's comments: _____

_____

_____

My contributions: _____

_____

_____

_____

Where I could have done better: _____

_____

_____

_____

Highlights of the game: _____

_____

_____

_____

_____

_____

Practice

Starting _____ until our next game on _____
                Day & Date   Day & Date

Coach's focus this week is: _____

_____

My focus this week is: _____

_____

How I feel looking ahead: _____

_____

What I think I can contribute to the team this week: _____

_____

My notes about this week's practice: _____

_____

_____

_____

_____

_____

_____

_____

Game Day

Game Date: _____ Game Time: _____

We played against: _____ Home ☐   Away ☐

Positions I played: _____ Final Score: _____

My summary: _____

_____

_____

_____

Coach's comments: _____

_____

_____

My contributions: _____

_____

_____

_____

Where I could have done better: _____

_____

_____

_____

Highlights of the game: _____

_____

_____

_____

_____

_____

Practice

Starting _____ until our next game on _____
                     Day & Date   Day & Date

Coach's focus this week is: _____

_____

_____

My focus this week is: _____

_____

_____

How I feel looking ahead: _____

_____

_____

What I think I can contribute to the team this week: _____

_____

_____

My notes about this week's practice: _____

_____

_____

_____

_____

_____

_____

_____

_____

Game Day

Game Date: _____ Game Time: _____

We played against: _____ Home ☐   Away ☐

Positions I played: _____ Final Score: _____

My summary: _____

_____

_____

_____

Coach's comments: _____

_____

_____

My contributions: _____

_____

_____

_____

Where I could have done better: _____

_____

_____

Highlights of the game: _____

_____

_____

_____

_____

_____

Practice

Starting _____ until our next game on _____
Day & Date   Day & Date

Coach's focus this week is: _____

_____

_____

My focus this week is: _____

_____

_____

How I feel looking ahead: _____

_____

_____

What I think I can contribute to the team this week: _____

_____

_____

My notes about this week's practice: _____

_____

_____

_____

_____

_____

_____

_____

_____

Game Day

Game Date: _____   Game Time: _____

We played against: _____   Home ☐   Away ☐

Positions I played: _____   Final Score: _____

My summary: _____

_____

_____

_____

Coach's comments: _____

_____

_____

My contributions: _____

_____

_____

Where I could have done better: _____

_____

_____

Highlights of the game: _____

_____

_____

_____

_____

_____

Practice

Starting _____ until our next game on _____
            Day & Date   Day & Date

Coach's focus this week is: _____

_____

_____

My focus this week is: _____

_____

_____

How I feel looking ahead: _____

_____

_____

What I think I can contribute to the team this week: _____

_____

_____

My notes about this week's practice: _____

_____

_____

_____

_____

_____

_____

_____

_____

_____

Game Day

Game Date: _____ Game Time: _____

We played against: _____ Home ☐   Away ☐

Positions I played: _____ Final Score: _____

My summary: _____

_____

_____

_____

Coach's comments: _____

_____

_____

My contributions: _____

_____

_____

Where I could have done better: _____

_____

_____

_____

Highlights of the game: _____

_____

_____

_____

_____

_____

Practice

Starting _____ until our next game on _____
           Day & Date   Day & Date

Coach's focus this week is: _____

_____

_____

My focus this week is: _____

_____

_____

How I feel looking ahead: _____

_____

_____

What I think I can contribute to the team this week: _____

_____

_____

My notes about this week's practice: _____

_____

_____

_____

_____

_____

_____

_____

_____

Game Day

Game Date: _____ Game Time: _____

We played against: _____ Home ☐ Away ☐

Positions I played: _____ Final Score: _____

My summary: _____

_____

_____

_____

Coach's comments: _____

_____

_____

My contributions: _____

_____

_____

_____

Where I could have done better: _____

_____

_____

_____

Highlights of the game: _____

_____

_____

_____

_____

_____

Practice

Starting _____ until our next game on _____
Day & Date   Day & Date

Coach's focus this week is: _____

_____

_____

My focus this week is: _____

_____

_____

How I feel looking ahead: _____

_____

_____

What I think I can contribute to the team this week: _____

_____

_____

My notes about this week's practice: _____

_____

_____

_____

_____

_____

_____

_____

_____

_____

Game Day

Game Date: _____ Game Time: _____

We played against: _____ Home ☐   Away ☐

Positions I played: _____ Final Score: _____

My summary: _____

_____

_____

_____

Coach's comments: _____

_____

_____

My contributions: _____

_____

_____

_____

Where I could have done better: _____

_____

_____

_____

Highlights of the game: _____

_____

_____

_____

_____

Practice

Starting _____ until our next game on _____
                Day & Date   Day & Date

Coach's focus this week is: _____

_____

My focus this week is: _____

_____

How I feel looking ahead: _____

_____

What I think I can contribute to the team this week: _____

_____

My notes about this week's practice: _____

_____

_____

_____

_____

_____

_____

_____

Game Day

Game Date: _____ Game Time: _____

We played against: _____ Home ☐   Away ☐

Positions I played: _____ Final Score: _____

My summary: _____

_____

_____

_____

Coach's comments: _____

_____

_____

My contributions: _____

_____

_____

Where I could have done better: _____

_____

_____

Highlights of the game: _____

_____

_____

_____

_____

Practice

Starting _____ until our next game on _____
           Day & Date   Day & Date

Coach's focus this week is: _____

_____

_____

My focus this week is: _____

_____

_____

How I feel looking ahead: _____

_____

_____

What I think I can contribute to the team this week: _____

_____

_____

My notes about this week's practice: _____

_____

_____

_____

_____

_____

_____

_____

Game Day

Game Date: _____ Game Time: _____

We played against: _____ Home ☐   Away ☐

Positions I played: _____ Final Score: _____

My summary: _____

_____

_____

_____

Coach's comments: _____

_____

_____

My contributions: _____

_____

_____

Where I could have done better: _____

_____

_____

Highlights of the game: _____

_____

_____

_____

_____

_____

Practice

Starting _____ until our next game on _____
                  Day & Date   Day & Date

Coach's focus this week is: _____

_____

My focus this week is: _____

_____

How I feel looking ahead: _____

_____

What I think I can contribute to the team this week: _____

_____

My notes about this week's practice: _____

_____

_____

_____

_____

_____

_____

_____

Game Day

Game Date: _____   Game Time: _____

We played against: _____ Home ☐   Away ☐

Positions I played: _____ Final Score: _____

My summary:

_____

_____

_____

Coach's comments: _____

_____

_____

My contributions: _____

_____

_____

Where I could have done better: _____

_____

_____

Highlights of the game: _____

_____

_____

_____

_____

Practice

Starting _____ until our next game on _____

Day & Date   Day & Date

Coach's focus this week is: _____

_____

My focus this week is: _____

_____

How I feel looking ahead: _____

_____

What I think I can contribute to the team this week: _____

_____

My notes about this week's practice: _____

_____

_____

_____

_____

_____

_____

_____

Game Day

Game Date: _____ Game Time: _____

We played against: _____ Home ☐ Away ☐

Positions I played: _____ Final Score: _____

My summary: _____

_____

_____

_____

Coach's comments: _____

_____

_____

My contributions: _____

_____

_____

Where I could have done better: _____

_____

_____

Highlights of the game: _____

_____

_____

_____

_____

Practice

Starting _____ until our next game on _____

Day & Date

Day & Date

Coach's focus this week is: _____

_____

_____

My focus this week is: _____

_____

_____

How I feel looking ahead: _____

_____

_____

What I think I can contribute to the team this week: _____

_____

_____

My notes about this week's practice: _____

_____

_____

_____

_____

_____

_____

_____

_____

Game Day

Game Date: _____ Game Time: _____

We played against: _____ Home ☐   Away ☐

Positions I played: _____ Final Score: _____

My summary: _____

_____

_____

_____

Coach's comments: _____

_____

_____

My contributions: _____

_____

_____

_____

Where I could have done better: _____

_____

_____

_____

Highlights of the game: _____

_____

_____

_____

_____

Practice

Starting _____ until our next game on _____
　　　　　　　Day & Date　　　　　　　　　　　　　　　　　　　　　　Day & Date

Coach's focus this week is: _____

_____

_____

My focus this week is: _____

_____

_____

How I feel looking ahead: _____

_____

_____

What I think I can contribute to the team this week: _____

_____

_____

My notes about this week's practice: _____

_____

_____

_____

_____

_____

_____

_____

Game Day

Game Date: _____ Game Time: _____

We played against: _____ Home ☐   Away ☐

Positions I played: _____ Final Score: _____

My summary: _____

_____

_____

_____

Coach's comments: _____

_____

_____

My contributions: _____

_____

_____

_____

Where I could have done better: _____

_____

_____

_____

Highlights of the game: _____

_____

_____

_____

_____

_____

Practice

Starting _____ until our next game on _____
                           Day & Date   Day & Date

Coach's focus this week is: _____

_____

_____

My focus this week is: _____

_____

_____

How I feel looking ahead: _____

_____

_____

What I think I can contribute to the team this week: _____

_____

_____

My notes about this week's practice: _____

_____

_____

_____

_____

_____

_____

_____

_____

What a season you've had!

You've used up 34 of your

worksheet sets.

There's one more after this page.

Use it to make as many

photocopies as you need

to complete your season.

Game Day

Game Date: .... Game Time: ....

We played against: .... Home ☐   Away ☐

Positions I played: .... Final Score: ....

My summary: ....

....

....

....

Coach's comments: ....

....

....

My contributions: ....

....

....

Where I could have done better: ....

....

....

Highlights of the game: ....

....

....

....

....

....

Practice

Starting _____ until our next game on _____
     Day & Date   Day & Date

Coach's focus this week is: _____

_____

_____

My focus this week is: _____

_____

_____

How I feel looking ahead: _____

_____

_____

What I think I can contribute to the team this week: _____

_____

_____

My notes about this week's practice: _____

_____

_____

_____

_____

_____

_____

_____

My
SOCCER
Season
Memories

Memories

Memories

Memories

Memories

About the Author

Karleen Tauszik writes books mostly for children ages 8 to 12. Her goal as an author is to get kids to LOVE reading. She is married to a pro-fessional ventriloquist and magician, and they live in the Tampa Bay area. Learn more about Karleen at her website, KarleenT.com.

Interested in other sports? Look for the rest of the "My Season" Journals by Karleen Tauszik:

My Softball Season

My Baseball Season

My Basketball Season

My Football Season

My Hockey Season

52598540R00053

Made in the USA
Middletown, DE
10 July 2019